せがわ せつこ キルトの世界

JAPANESE QUILT ART

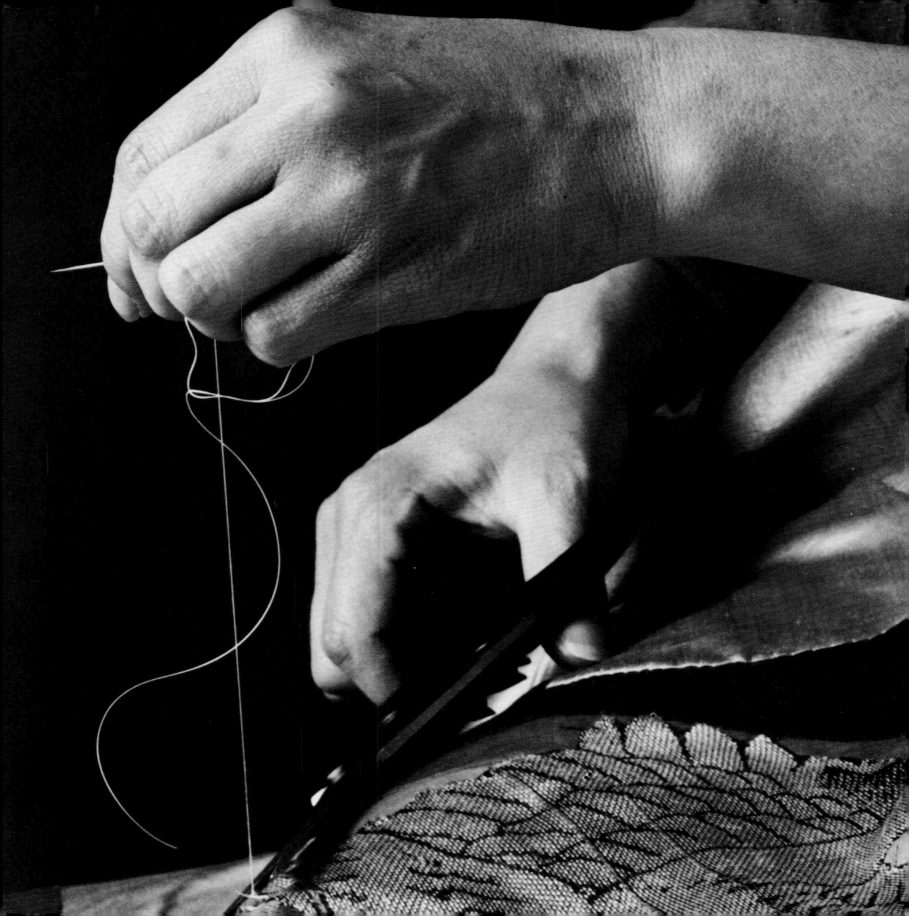

せがわ せつこ キルトの世界

JAPANESE QUILT ART

by Setsuko Segawa

Published by Mitsumura Suiko Shoin

Kyoto Japan

せがわせつこ著

京都　光村推古書院刊

Published by Mitsumura Suiko Shoin Co., Ltd. Kyoto Japan
© 1985 Setsuko Segawa
Prologue by Tetsuro Kitamura, Takeshi Ohtaka
Design by Takeshi Ohtaka
Photographs by Nobuo Kanemoto
First Edition June 1985
ISBN4-8381-0080-9

目　次
CONTENTS

あとがき

装幀・レイアウト   大高 猛
Design   Takeshi Ohtaka

撮影   兼本延夫
Photographs   Nobuo Kanemoto

序 文
PREFACE

作品集刊行に寄せて

共立女子大学教授　北村哲郎

　私がモラやパッチワークの面白さや美しさに初めて接したのは、今から20年程前になります。それはアメリカとカナダで行われた展覧会に随伴して、半年程彼地に滞在中、暇をみて歩き廻った博物館等での出合いでした。その頃、日本ではそれらの紹介は全くされておらず、持ち帰ったモラの資料を「こんな美しいものがある」という名前で展観をした程でした。それが昭和50年代に入ると、雑誌等にも取りあげられ、広く人々に知られるようになりました。特にパッチワークは仕事そのものが、特別な技術を要するものではないだけに、急速に普及し、教室が開かれたり、教本が出版されたり、展覧会も催されるなど、一つの流行となってきました。パッチワークに関しては、日本は今やアメリカに次いで盛んな国と言えるのではないでしょうか。

　もともとパッチワークは衣服が財産の一つとされ裂類が甚だ貴重な時代の知恵が生みだしたものでしたから、裂のあり余っている現在では、全く顧みられなくとも不思議はないのに、それが逆に流行しているのは面白い現象と言えましょう。わが国でも江戸時代末のきびしい倹約令の最中に、高価な総絞りの反物数種を小裂に裁ってはぎ合わせ、如何にもあまり裂を綴って作ったようにみせかけた振袖が現存しています。これらは武家という権力者に対する、経済力を持った町人の痛烈な皮肉、揶揄とみられますが、現在のパッチワークの流行もある意味では大量消費時代への逆説的反映と言えなくもなさそうです。

　もっとも、今日のアメリカにおけるパッチワークは、仕事のやりかたこそ昔と変わりませんが、小裂の集合による色彩効果や色面構成の意匠、異素材の組み合わせに芸術的独創性を求める現代芸術の一分野とされています。つまり、手芸や民俗芸術の域を脱して、伝統に立脚した現代美術に位置づけされていると言ってよいでしょう。

　せがわせつこさんの仕事もまさにそれで、パッチワーク、キルト、アップリケ等の技法を駆使して、芸術表現に取り組んでいます。彼女の創造の世界は大変広く、幾何構成の基本的なものから、所謂クレージーな非象形の世界、メルヘンの世界、抽象の世界、そしてアップリケを加えた自由構成の世界と大きな拡がりを持っています。彼女は非常に色彩感覚に優れた人ですが、近年は材質を異にする多様な日本の織物の裂を素材に、自由構成の布面を表現することに力を注ぎ、日本的抒情に溢れた彼女自身の世界を作り上げつつあるように見受けられます。彼女は和紙への挑戦のように、今後もさまざまな可能性の探求を続け、美の創造に努めてゆくことでしょうから、将来が嘱望される作家です。

PREFACE

Tetsuro Kitamura

I first became acquainted with Mora and patchwork quilts when I stayed in the States and Canada about twenty years ago. Because they had not been introduced to Japan until that time, I was so impressed with their intricate design and beauty that I showed research paper about them when I came back to Japan titled "There are such beautiful things."

Since fifty's of Showa period patchwork quilts have become popular rapidly among Japanese people.

I could say that Japan is second only to the States in appreciation of patchwork quilts Originally patchwork was given at birth when fabric was a very precious commodity. Therefore, it is an interesting phenomenon that patchwork quilts are very popular in the present state of prosperity.

In the States, today's patchwork is evaluated as a field of modern art, seeking artistic originality through color effect, forming design by putting together small pieces of fabric and combination of different types of fabric. That is to say, it takes its place in modern art based on tradition surpassing the sphere of handicraft or folk art.

Setsuko Segawa's quilt works are exactly what I have mentioned. She has been extending her artistic expression making full use of such techniques as patchwork, quilting, applique and other related art media.

Her creative subjects range widely from the basic geometric pattern, so called "crazy" irregularly shaped patches, fantasy style, abstract to free style with applique. She has an excellent sense of color.

Recently she is attempting to increase expression using various Japanese texture to build up her original world full of Japanese lyric feeling.

As she attempts to use Japanese paper as a material I believe that she is continuing to strive for various possibilities to create beauty. She shows great promise as an artist.

発刊によせて

グラフィックデザイナー
大高 猛

15年前、大阪で開かれた日本万国博のアメリカ館で、アメリカン・パッチワークを観た時の爽やかで感動的な印象は、今でも新鮮である。そのキメ細かい手仕事から、アメリカ人の合理性と忍耐力、さらに大陸的開拓精神の力強さを読みとることが出来た事で、器用さにかけては、と自負していた日本人の鼻がしらを、へし折られた思いだった——。それは古い衣服、シーツやカーテンなどを細かくカットして、丁寧に継ぎ合わせ、新しい布地に変貌させている。その長い時間と、手間暇かけて作り上げたキルトは、家族や隣人からの感嘆の言葉に、肩をこらせた苦労も吹き飛んだであろう情景が目に浮かぶようで、縫い込められた生地の一片からは、当時のファッションや、生活環境も想像される。同時にキルトは市民生活の歴史の証言者といえるだろう——。

パッチワークは一世紀以上の歴史を経て、今日、キルトアートにまで発展した。

アーティストせがわせつこは、この華麗なキルトの世界に着目した。さらに彼女は欧米のキルト文化から、日本の伝統芸術との結合を考え、日本古来の着物裂生地、染裂生地を活かして、古典美を現代アートへと、その表現の世界を広げている。彼女は一見、細身で小柄だが忍耐強く、キルトに向ける執念は並ではない。日本の伝統的裂生地をこよなく愛し、多彩な裂生地を絵具に、ひと刺しひと刺しの針を絵筆としてキルトを完成させる。

既存の裂地は一瞬にして創造的芸術に変身する。私はこれらの作品をジャパネスク・キルトアートと呼びたい。

彼女がいつしか、このジャパネスク・キルトアートを不動のものにする日に向かって努力されんことを望みたい。

PREFACE

Takeshi Ohtaka

At the last Osaka World Fair fifteen years ago, there were American patchworks exhibited in the US Pavilion. Even now their delightful impression remains fresh in my memory. We could see the rational perseverance as well as the vigorous pioneer spirit of the American continent from such delicate handicraft. This almost humbled our pride and self-confidence that the Japanese is cleverer with his hand. Used clothes, bedsheets, drapes, etc....cut into small patches were carefully stitched together into a piece of new cloth. It came into my mind how the quiltwork thus created with much labor and time drew a great admiration of other family members and neighbours, making the designer forget all her efforts and stiff shoulders.

Every patch of the cloth suggests us a particular fashion and life of the past. In this meaning, the quiltwork is a witness of the history. The patchwork quilt has a history of over a century before it was developed to the modern quilt art.

The artist Setsuko Segawa has got interested in the gorgeous world of quiltwork. With a view to combine the Western Quilt culture with the traditional art of Japan, she has made use of patches of Kimono cloth and printed cloth traditional to Japan to extend her world of expression from the classic beauty to the modern art. At a first glance, she is small and slender but she is patient enough to be dedicated to the Quilt Art with an incomparable spirit.

She completes the quiltwork affectionately stich by stich using patches of traditional Japanese cloth, which she is very fond of, as paints and a needle as the brush. Mere patches of cloth are thus instantly converted into a creative artwork. It can be named "The Japanese Quilt Art". I hope that she will steadily strive for her goal to firmly establish the Japanese Quilt Art.

13

自己表現とキルト歴史

せがわせつこ

Toward Self Expression
by Setsuko Segawa

裂にはさまざまな表情があり、絵具では表現しがたい面白さがある。素材の違いにより同じ色でも異質な色に見えてくる。長年にわたりパッチワークを手がけてきたが、「裂」には単なる布といいきれない何かがある。

つぎ合わせた裂にも一つの歴史がある。世界の各地で生まれたパッチワークの歴史は古く、原始時代に狩をした人々が動物の皮をつなぎ合わせたことを、もっとも原始的な手法と考えれば、現在のすべての手法の源といえるかもしれない。又、6世紀から9世紀の間には、シルクロードに位置したインドで奉納物や旗が発見されたり、11世紀から12世紀の頃には、十字軍が中東やエジプト等からパッチワークを持ち帰ったといわれている。又、初期のキルトは、武具の中に用いられていたが、14世紀にヨーロッパを襲った大寒波の時、人々は衣類や寝具をキルトで作り寒さをしのいだという。

ヨーロッパからアメリカへ伝わったのは、17世紀の初め、ニューイングランド地方への移民によるものだといわれる。当時、新しい布を手にすることは非常に困難で、どんな布きれも有効に利用するという考え方は、開拓民にとって極めて自然な成りゆきだったといえる。布が手に入るようになると、布を大きく切ったり、選択して用いるようになり、独立戦争の頃から南部で芸術的な発展を遂げたといわれる。それから100年を経た南北戦争の後、ピースドキルト、アップリケが北部や西部に伝わったといわれている。南北戦争前後、機械織の毛布類が普及すると、これらのものが好まれるようになり、キルトは実用を離れて装飾性が強くなり、ぜいたくな布が使われ、刺しゅうで飾られたビクトリアン調のものが復活したといわれる。

独立戦争100年祭の頃には、機械化によって人々の需要や習慣は大きく変わり、キルトは一部の愛好家の間で趣味の形として残されたが、20世紀になってからフォーク・アートとして周期的なリバイバルを見せた。このような形でアメリカ・ヨーロッパに限らず、日本で、また世界のあらゆる国々で、名称は違うが生まれ育ったといえるのではないだろうか。

現在のパッチワークキルトは、近代抽象画に等しい芸術手工芸に育ち上がり、フォーク・アートの域にとどまらず、その独創的なデザインや色彩は現代美術にも通じるものと評価されている。

私も5年程前までは、幾何学的なピースドキルトを生徒たちに指導したり、制作もしてきたが、もともと私はキルトによって、また裂によって自分を表現したいと考えていた。指導してきた生徒たちも、ピースドキルトに関しては、どこに出ても押しも押されもしないくらいに成長してくれたということもある。私自身、本来、キルト・アートやオブジェを目指していたので、生徒たちが育ってくれたことで私自身選択した道を進み始めた。「裂」といちがいに言いきれない何かによって——。

確かに材質は布に違いないのだが、非常に多くの可能性を秘めた布たちは、使われるのを望んでいるように思われて、私は裂さがしをする。古都の街を肩に大きなボストンをかけ、両手に裂を入れた紙袋をさげて、気に入った裂が見つかるまで歩きつづけ

る。思うように一カ所では集まらない。重さなど忘れ、まるで恋人にでも逢えるような気持でそれらを探し歩く——。

デザインする時にじっと裂を見ていると、「私をここに使ってください。」と言っているような気がする。その時、私の頭には出来上がりの実物大が見えてくる——。私は幼い頃からカラーの夢をみていた。最初は他の人たちも同じだと思い込んでいたがやがて違いが分かると、自分が成長してカラーに関わる仕事に携わりはじめるまで、そのことを人に言えなかった——。何故ならば、私の幼い頃は、カラーの夢をみる時は精神的に非常に疲れているとか、その他さまざまなジンクスがあったから——。

知人であり信頼もしている著名な心理学者松原教授に相談すると、彼は微笑みながら答えてくれた。「カラーに深く関わっている貴女が、カラーの夢をみるのは極く当たり前のこと、小さい頃にみていたのは、その頃からカラーに対するインスピレーションがあったのだろう。」と。それからは前以上に色を使う楽しさが増して、デザインするのも思うようになった。もちろん今でもカラーの夢は出てくる。時折り夜中に目がさめ、夢の光景、色、構図をメモすることもしばしばである。

単なるパッチワークで終わらせたくないと思う自分の信念を守り通すについて、私にはさまざまな人間模様があった——。人と人との出逢い、喜び、不安、怒り、悲しみ、別れ、希望、それ等のすべてが私を大きく成長させてくれたように思える。時々、信念をまげそうになると自分に呼びかける。「もし

かしてなんて考えたらいけない！止まってはいけない！まして戻ろうと思ったらいけない！」。迷っている時は自分なりに判断しチャレンジしてみる。一度で無理だと分かったら何回もチャレンジする。何もせずにただ迷っているより自分なりに少しは成長してゆけるような気がする。信念をもつこと、我ではなく、その信念をいかにして貫くかは、人生において困難なことだけれど——。

ここまで成長できたのは、私の意志の強さもあるけれど、私にとってのよきブレーン達、私を信頼して10年近くもついて来てくれたP．Q．M．A．のメンバー、そして友人等によって支えられたともいえるだろう——。また作品展を見ていただき、初めてお会いする方から「蔵の中に眠っている裂がある、お役に立てば…」と送っていただくこともある。私は送られて来た裂をよみがえらせる意味で作品にする。その方々が喜んでくださったのが目に浮かんでくる。このような方々も私を育ててくださった陰の協力者である。

幸いなことに、日本には外国では入手が困難な素材が豊富に揃っている。私はこれ等の材質を生かしより日本的な感覚で、古典調、シュール的なもの、コラージュ風のものなど、多彩に表現する上で、これらの豊富な素材を自由に選べることは非常にありがたいと思う。

長年手がけてきた基礎的なものの上で、自分を表現したいと思う夢を抱きつづけ、裂を単なる布と見ず、色と見て多様に使い分けてきた。従ってデザインはもちろん大切であるが、私は色彩に重点をおい

ている。世界各地の特色を生かし、東洋と西洋の文
化と歴史をミックスさせ、なおそれにナイズされる
ことなく、日本のもの、自分のものとして消化し、
独自な表現をすることに努めてきた。また元来、人
間のもつ多面性、両極性は私の中にもあり、それに
逆らわずにデザインした場合、初めて見る方は全く
異質な作品のように思われるだろうが、これも正直
な自己表現と考えて発表したい。

裂や糸などすべてを絵具、針を絵筆と考え、絵具
で表現しがたい何かを、それ等によって創り出して
ゆきたいと考えている。

パッチワークは、必ずしも布と布とでなければな
らないというルールはないと思う。余りにも既成概
念に捉われすぎていると新しいものは生まれてこな
いのではないだろうか──。私がリーダーをしてい
るP．Q．M．A．のPは、パッチワークのPでもあ
るが、もう一つの意味をもっている。Progressive
（現実にとどまることなく常に前進する）という意
味も含めている。私自身この言葉の意味も非常に好
きだが、すべてにおいて通じる言葉だと思う。もち
ろん自分の置かれた立場を十分理解してのことだと
思うが──。

今日のキルターは、用と美とのターニングポイン
トに立っているのではないだろうか──。機能性に
重点をおく人、アートを目指す人、さまざまだと思
う。それ等はすべて、その人達個人が選択すること
であるから、どちらがすばらしいとは言い切れない
ような気がする。それは私が教えているメンバー達
にも言えることだが、私は敢えて「多くの作品やも

のを見なさい。多くのことを知った上で、本当に自
分がやりたいキルトに進みなさい」と常に言いつづ
けている。作品にしてもカラーにしても、ものの見
方に幅が出てくるのではないだろうか──。

私自身、キルトデザイナーではあるが、インテリ
アのコーディネイター、フラワーデザイナー、料理
研究家としても、カラーのバランスや器との調和を
重視している。そのような中で、毎週、東京と大阪
を往復する新幹線の車中で、ふと自分の思ったこと
を書きとめ、ゆっくりした時に詩集にまとめたりも
する。これらが今日の私にとってどれほどプラスに
なり、また私を成長させたかは、知る人は知るだろ
う──。

今でもそうだが、違った角度からキルトを見て、
用と美との接点を追求しながら、自由に創作してゆ
きたいと考えている。

空──
　　流れる　流れる　いわしぐも
　　一秒ごとに変わってゆく
　　変わる──変わる　見ているうちに
　　スクリーンのように変わってゆく
　　まるで私の心のように
　　一瞬……光がさす……美しい！

海──
　　おだやかな海
　　ギラギラとした青い海
　　自然を破滅させるような海
　　こおりつきそうな冷たい海──
　　どれも好きだなァ

川──
　　川のように流れて　　いたいなァ──
　　さらさらと小川のせせらぎみたいに
　　岩にぶつかる清流のように
　　又　あるときは
　　濁流のように激しくなって
　　大きな海へ流れて　　みたいなァ

Cloth is expressive and of greater interest than painted descriptions. Depending on the type of fabrics, even the same color looks different. For a long time, I have been designing patchwork quilts and have found that "fragments" — a piece of fabric—are something much more than just a cloth.

Patchworked fragments have a story. Patchwork quilts throughout the world have a long history. As a primitive way of patchworking, ancient hunters put together animal hides, so we can say that is the origin of today's techniques. Between the sixth century and ninth century, patchworked dedicated objects and flags were discovered in the Silk Road area of India. Around the eleventh and twelfth centuries, the Crusades took quilted works back from the Middle East or Egypt, it is said. In the earlier ages, quilts were used in arms but in the fourteenth century when Europe was attacked by a great cold wave, European people put together cloth to make garments or bedclothes and took shelter from the coldness.

It is said that patchwork quilts were introduced to America from Europe by immigrants in New England in the beginning of the seventeenth century. Because it was very difficult to get new clothes in those days, consequently, they had to use whichever cloth or fragment they had as effectively as they could. Coming to the time when they could get cloth easily, they cut them widely or chose as they liked, and Patchwork quilts developed greatly in terms of artistic development in the South around the time of the Revolutionary War. A hundred years later, after the Civil War, pieced quilts and applique were introduced to the North and the West. Before and after the Civil War, various kinds of machine woven blankets were spread and became popular. Patchwork quilts at this time were separate from practical use and only for decorative use. Victorian design embelished with embroidery was also restored in this era.

Around the year of the centennial anniversary of the Revolutionary War people's demands or customs had changed greatly through mechanization. As a result, quilts were left as a hobby among just quilts lovers (quilters). In the twentieth century, quilts were revived periodically as a folk art. Not only in Europe and America, but in Japan and various countries in the world, even though they are called different names, patchwork quilts were born and brought up in each country in this way, I would like to say.

Today's patchwork quilts have progressed to the artistic handicraft equivalent to modern abstract art, and outside the sphere of folk art they are evaluated in their unique design and coloring, with the same sense as modern art.

I had been teaching and making geometric pieced quilts until five years ago. But originally I had wanted to express myself through quilts and cloth. My disciples became unchallenged as pieced quilters, so I aimed at making quilt art or "objets d'art", therefore myself started walking my chosen way.

Cloth, to me, is not just material, because I always associate it with lots of possibilities. I feel cloth seems to be looking to be by me. Thinking of that, I walk around in historic cities looking for fragments of cloth until I find all the ones that please me, carrying a big bag on my shoulder and paper bags full of cloth in each hand. I seldom gather all of the cloth I want in one area. I am looking for cloth as if I am looking for my lover, forgetting the heaviness of the bags.

When I form a design and stare at the fragments it seems that they tell me to use them here and there. Then I can visualize my finished quilt work in full size. Since I was a child, I have dreamt in color. At first I believed that everybody did. However once I knew that I was different from others, I could not tell people about my dreams until I was involved in the work related to colors. That was because when I dreamt in color in my childhood, I was very tired mentally and a colored dream meant various jinx.

One of my reliable acquaintances, celebrated psychologist professor Matsubara, told me that I was so involved in color that it is natural for me to dream in color and that colored dream in my childhood indicated that I had inspiration towards colors even then. Since then I have enjoyed coloring much more than before and can form a design as I desire. Of course even now I dream in color, and sometimes wake up in the middle of the night to draw the scene, color and composition of the dream I have just dreamt.

I don't let my work end up as mere patchwork quilt, and in the process of keeping this belief, I've had many experiences, encounters, partings, pleasure, anxiety, anger, sorrow, hope, etc. These things made me grow greatly, I think. When I am about to yield and weaken my belief, I tell myself that I don't have to think about failing, stopping or going back. When I am at a loss, I judge it in my way and challenge it over and over even though I know it is impossible at the time. Rather than be at a loss doing nothing, I feel like making slight progress by challenging myself. Having my belief, keeping it, without it becoming ego is difficult in my life, though.

It is not only because I have a strong will, but because I was supported by my good brains, members of P.Q.M.A.(Patchwork Quilt Association) who have relied on and followed me for about ten years, and friends, that I can grow greatly. Furthermore, there is a woman, who comes to my exhibition and whom I have never seen before, she sends me antique cloth stored in her warehouse with her message that she would be happy if they are useful. I make quilts using that cloth intending to enliven them. I can just see her being pleased. Such a woman is also a hidden collaborator.

Fortunately I can see a large selection of fabrics in Japan which I cannot get in foreign countries. How thankful I am for a free choice from this abundance of fabric in order to express myself in a very Japanese sense and classical tone, surrealistic style, or collage style etc, putting them to good use.

I have entertained a hope that I could express myself based upon the fundamentals. I have taken fragments not just for the cloth, but for colors, and used them properly. Accordingly, not to mention designs, I make much more of colors. I have also tried to express myself making the most of the characteristics of other countrie's cultures, understanding the culture, and history of the East and the West simultaneously and learning it so as to be part of mine without westernizing it. Like all humans, I have inside me a polyhedric personality and all the extremes of feeling. A design which forms according to this character seems to people who first see it that this is quite different from the work of others, I suppose. But I would like to make public my works as honest self expression.

Assuming fragments, cloths and threads to be paints and needles to be paintbrushes, I would like to create something I cannot express by paint with them.

In my point of view, there is no rule that patchwork should be composed necessarily of cloth and cloth. If we are trapped deeply by our stereotypes, we cannot invent new things completely different from all others. I am a head of P.Q.M.A. a capital P is the abbreviation of patchwork and also has another meaning, progressive, moving forward continuously. I myself like this word and the meaning very much, and understand it as applied in many cases, provided I think of my position throughly.

I wonder if today's quilter is standing on the turning point between practicality and beauty. Some people lay stress on function, others on artistic effect. I cannot assert which is better because the choice is up to the individual. I might say the same thing to my disciples I am teaching. I keep telling them to appreciate as many as they can and choose the quilt they really want after they know plenty of things. By doing that I am sure they get broader perspectives of works or colors.

As well as a quilt designer, as a interior coordinator, flower designer and cooking adviser I attach importance on color balance and the vessel's harmony. Every week I go and come back from Tokyo to Osaka, and during the time on the bullet train I write poems and collect them for a book later. I write down what come to my mind and collect them for a poetic works later when I relax. These things are an asset for me and help me grow.

I think of my work creatively, reaching a point of contact between practicality and beauty, looking at quilts from a different angle.

❶水 仙
Suisen
860 x 1170mm

❷青　梅
Ao Ume
820 x 1130mm

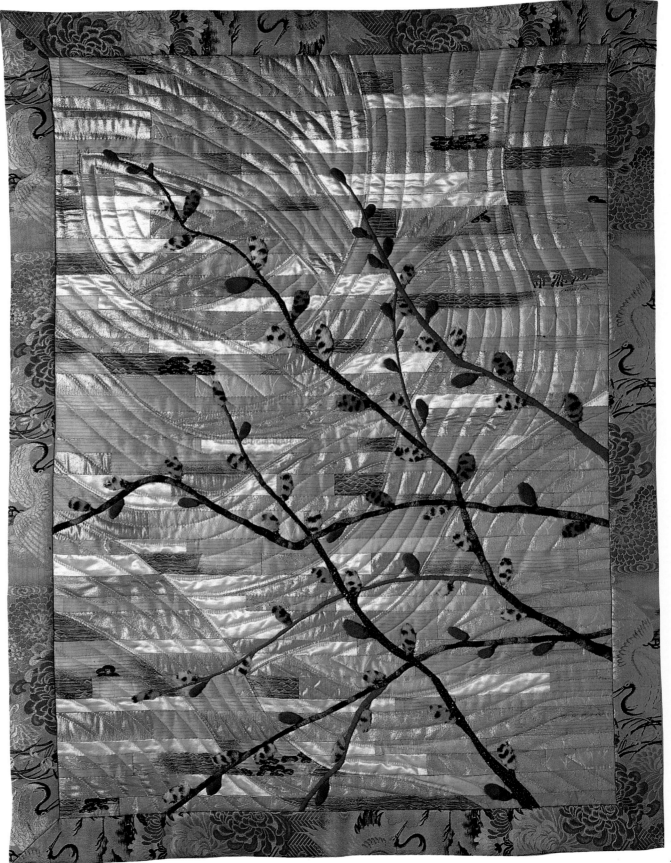

❸猫 柳
Neko Yanagi
1150 x 860mm

❹山　吹
Yamabuki
820 x 1180mm

❺木 蓮
Mokuren
1190 x 900mm

29

❻ 藤
Fuji
1120 x 900mm

❼牡 丹
Botan
890 x 1180mm

❽紫陽花
Ajisai
800 x 1150mm

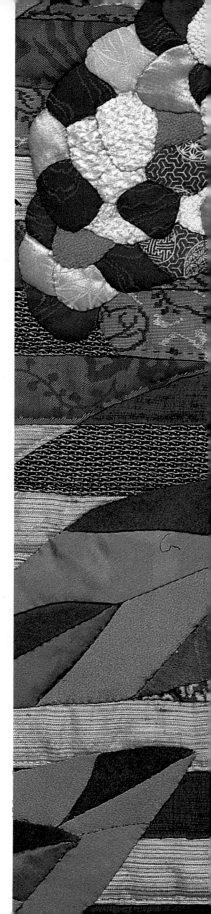

❾部分
detail

⓾ 菖 蒲
Shôbu
820 x 1150mm

34

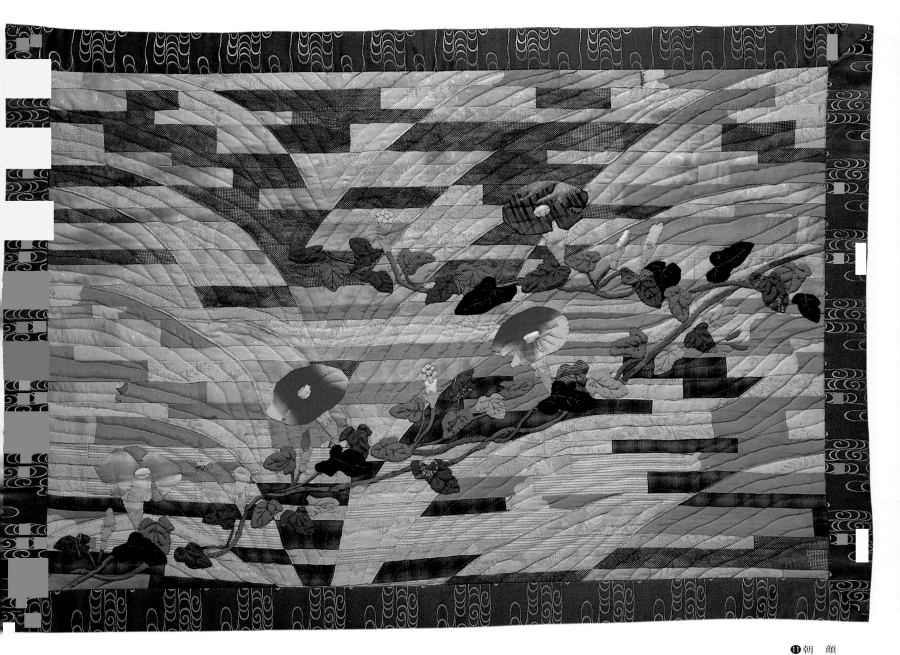

⓫朝　顔
Asagao
800 x 1130mm

⓬鉄　線
Tessen
870 × 1180mm

⓭ 向日葵
Himawari
820 x 1150mm

❶❹ 彼岸花
Higanbana
820 × 1120mm

⓯紫式部
Murasaki Shikibu
1120 x 820mm

⑯ 蒲
Gama
1150 x 1530mm

⓱椿
Tsubaki
860 x 1170mm

❶⓮イメージ・オブ・北斎
Image of Hokusai
Image de Hokusai
830 x 1130mm

⓴寒秋のシンフォニー
Symphony
Symphonie
980 x 1480mm

44

㉑ 大和路
Yamatoji
960 x 1280mm

45

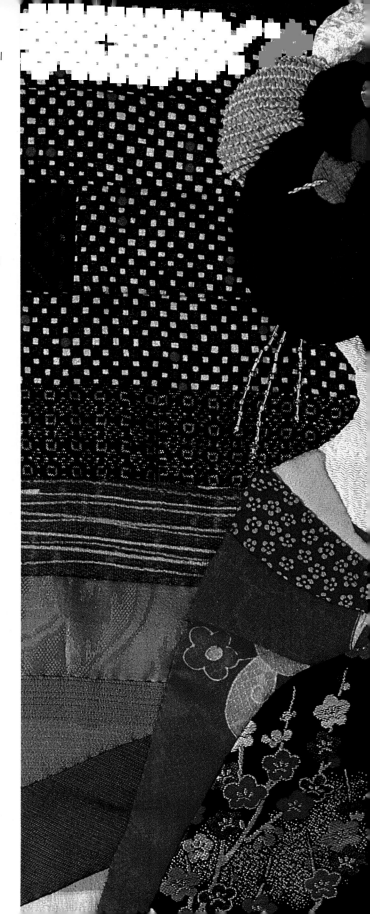

❷❷ 京　都
Kyoto
1200 x 810mm

❷❹古 壺
Antique vase
Vase antique
1230 x 810mm

㉕渡　海
Migrating birds
Oiseaux de passage
700 x 1000mm

剣
大野城市剣道連盟

氣迫
那珂川町
那珂川町長 生松仁志

創立十周年記念
剣心
筑紫野 山口剣友会

心動不
国士舘大学 剣道部

晩氣
國士舘大學 總長柴田龍夫

武振
太宰府振武会創立三十周年記念

心動不
国士舘大学 剣道部

殺一禅剣

躍進
第二回高校対抗

剣
大野城市剣道連盟

剣
大野城市剣道連盟

❷❼乱　舞
Wild dance
Danse sauvage
610 x 910mm

❷❻気　迫
Determination
Caractère
2100 x 2100mm

㉘迷　夢
Wandering dream
Rêve errant
1860 x 1430mm

❷❾ 波濤 I
Billow-I
Grandes vagues-I
950 x 680mm

㉚ 波濤 II
Billow-II
Grandes vagues-II
930 x 680mm

㉛ 部分
detail

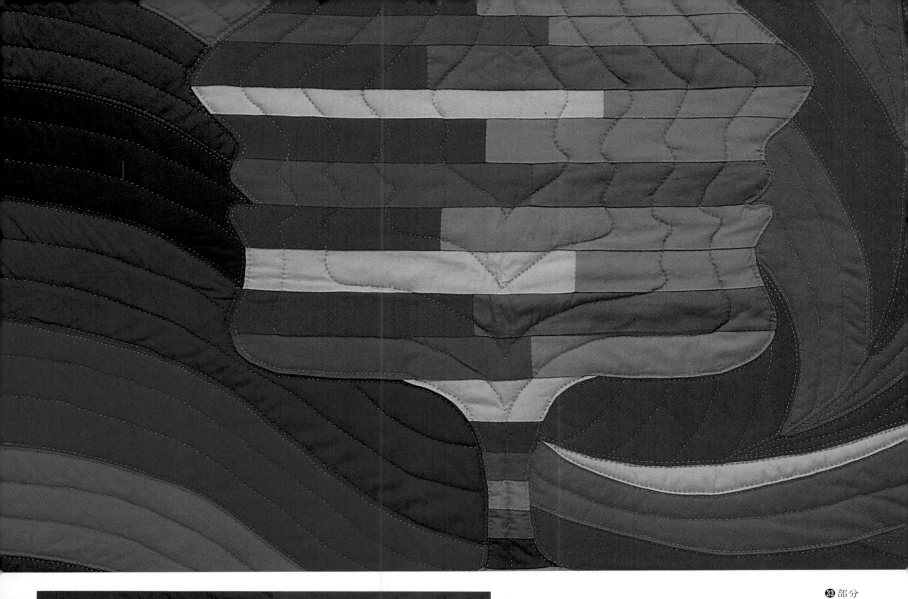

❸❷ 暗暗裏
Emotions
830 x 1200mm

❸❺ 波動Ⅱ
Flux-Ⅱ
700 x 1000mm

❸❹ 波動Ⅰ
Flux-Ⅰ
700 x 1000mm

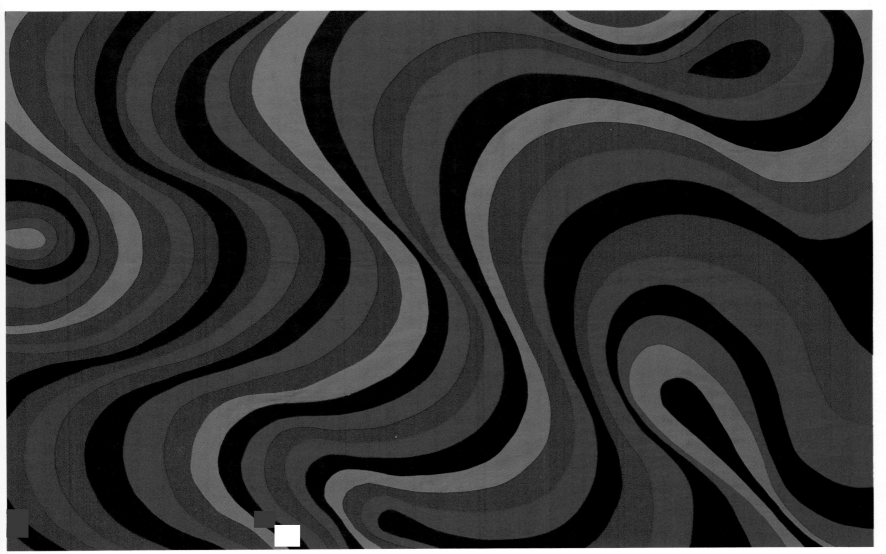

㊲ 部分
detail

㊱ 沈　黙
Silent
Impavide
1190 x 670mm

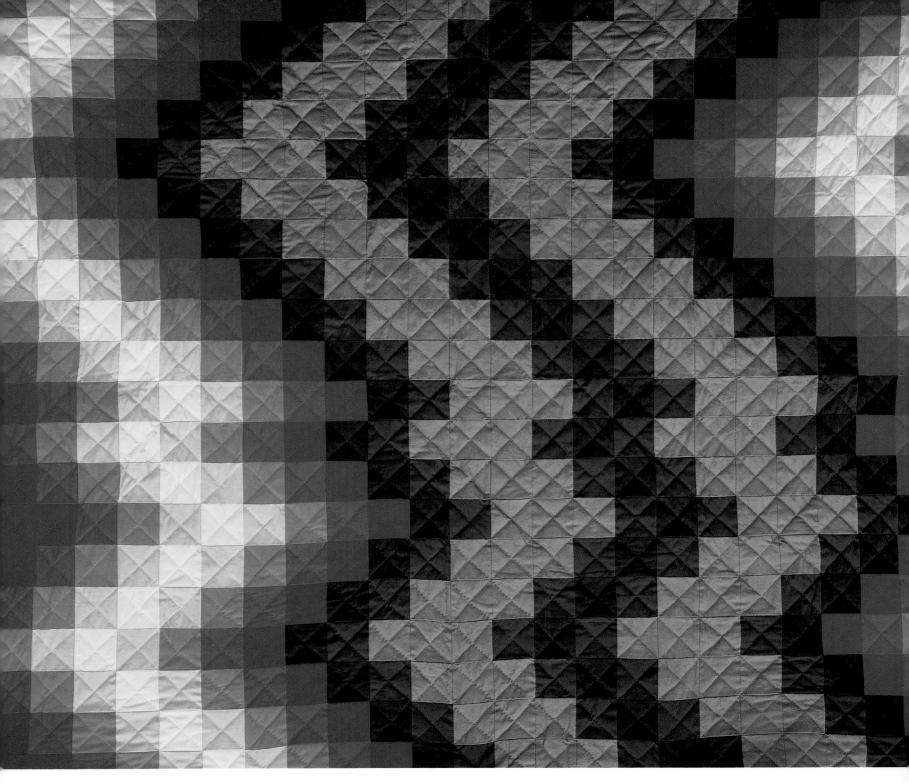

❸❽激動の予感
Passionate
Passionné
1960 x 2360mm

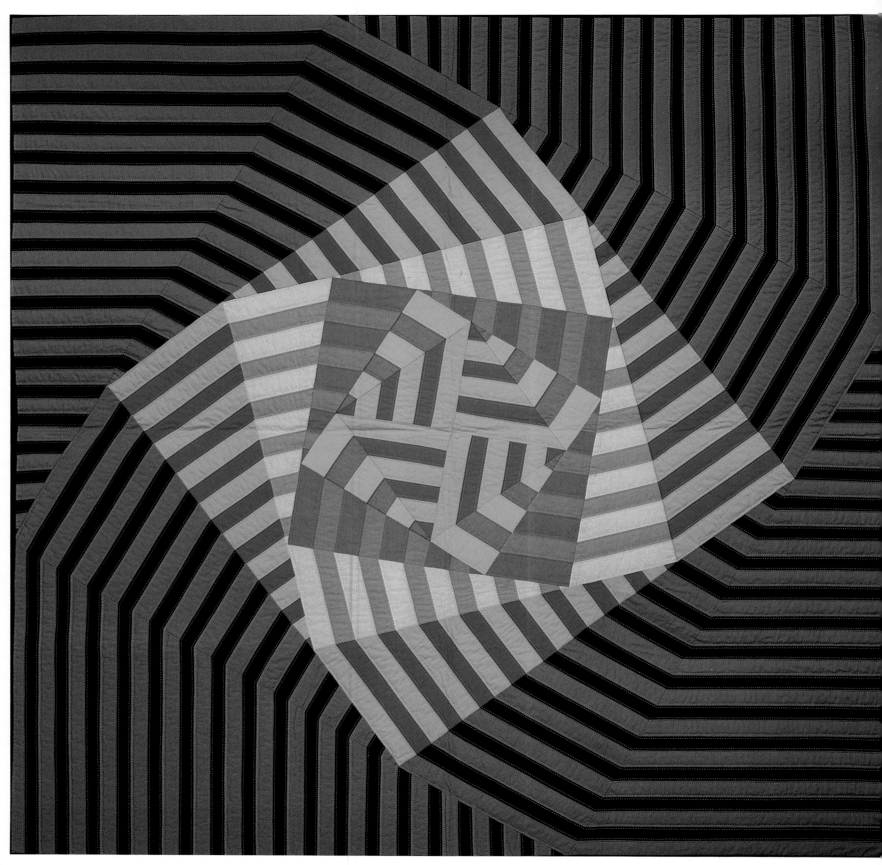

⑩ 活　動
Movements
Mouvements
700 x 1000mm

㊴ 紆余曲折
Destinies
Destinées entrelacées
1380 x 1380mm

42 紫の楽き
Violet echo
Echo violet
690 x 990mm

41 トロピカル・モーニング
Tropical morning
Aube tropicale
1660 x 1580mm

63

❹❹ 海星 II
Starfish-II
Etoile de mer-II
700 x 1000mm

❹❸ 海星 I
Starfish-I
Etoile de mer-I
760 x 1100mm

❹❺物体 X
Material
Matière

1470 x 1700mm

人魚の海
The sea and the mermaids
Les sirènes et la mer
700 × 1000mm

❹❼ バード・ミーティング
Birds meeting
Entre oiseaux
880 x 1620mm

❹❾ 飛翔 II
Leaping to the sky-II
Saut dans le ciel-II
1180 x 860mm

❹❽ 飛翔 I
Leaping to the sky-I
Saut dans le ciel-I
1030 x 730mm

㊿ 流　浪
Wanderings
Longs voyages
1320 x 1080mm

⑤1 感　覚
Sense
Bon goût
960 x 1350mm

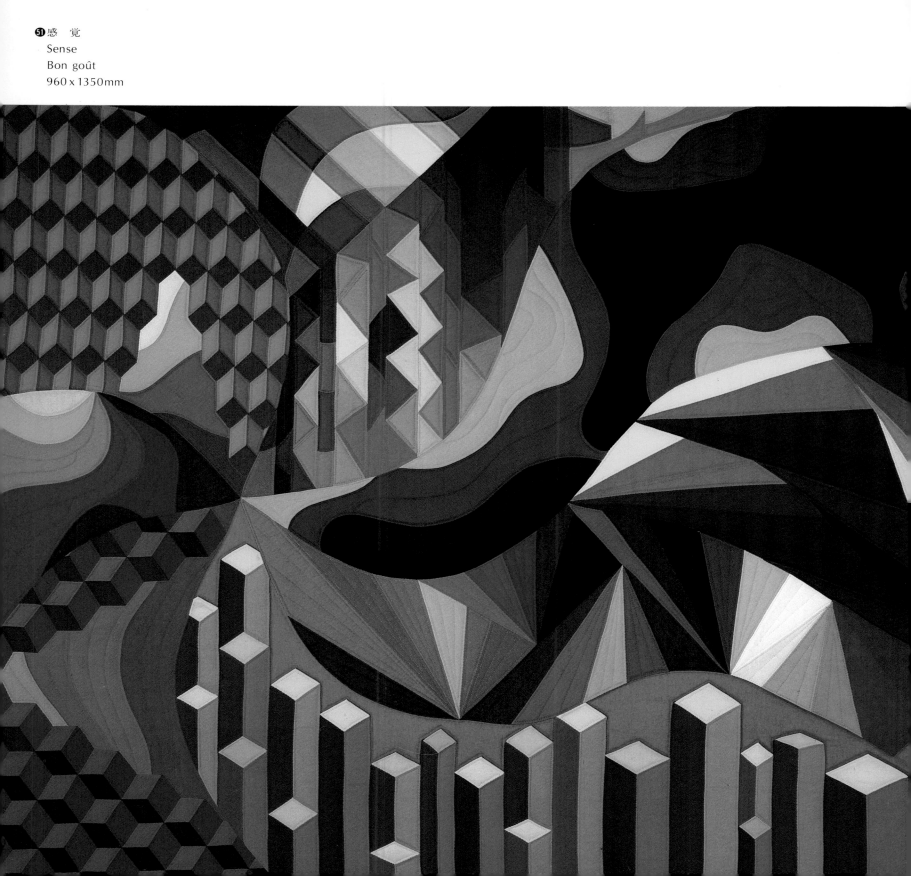

52 都会・不安・期待・成功
City-Anxiety, hope, success
Ville-anxiété, espoir, succès
1610 x 1680mm

73

❸ 層 層
Strata
Couches

810 x 1110mm

尖　塔
Pinnacle
Clocher
1240 x 2000 mm

❺❺無限Ⅰ
Infinitude-Ⅰ
Infini-Ⅰ
710 x 980mm

❺❻無限Ⅱ
Infinitude-Ⅱ
Infini-Ⅱ
620 x 940mm

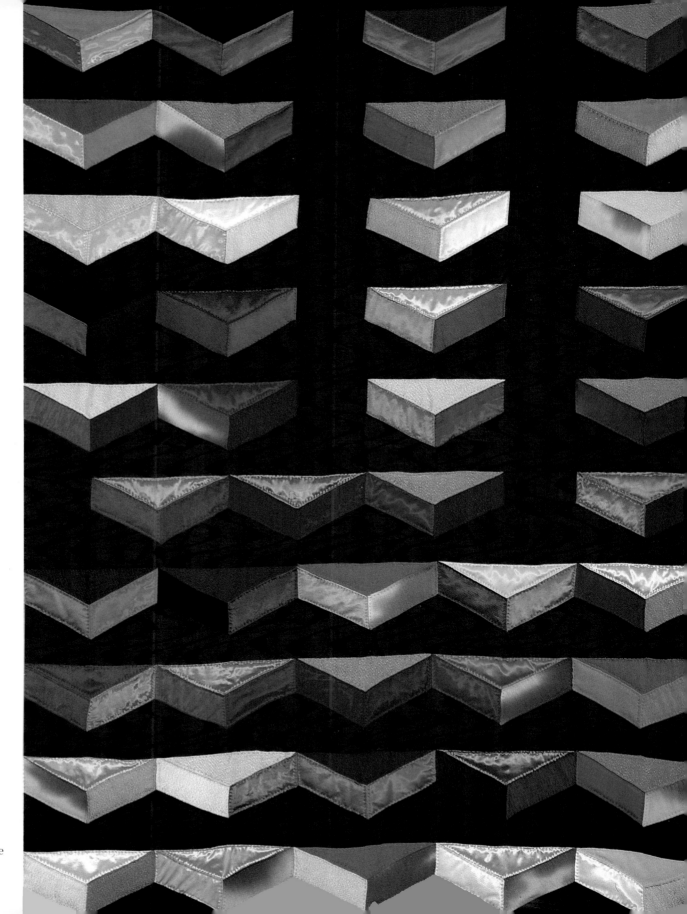

㊼ トライアングル・ステージ
Triangle stage
Progression triangulaire
1350 x 950mm

❺❽ ダイアモンド・カット
Diamond cut
Losanges
690 x 680mm

⑤⑨連 子
Lattice window
Fenêtre
540 x 770mm

㉑ 無　題
No title
Non titré
2190 x 2500mm

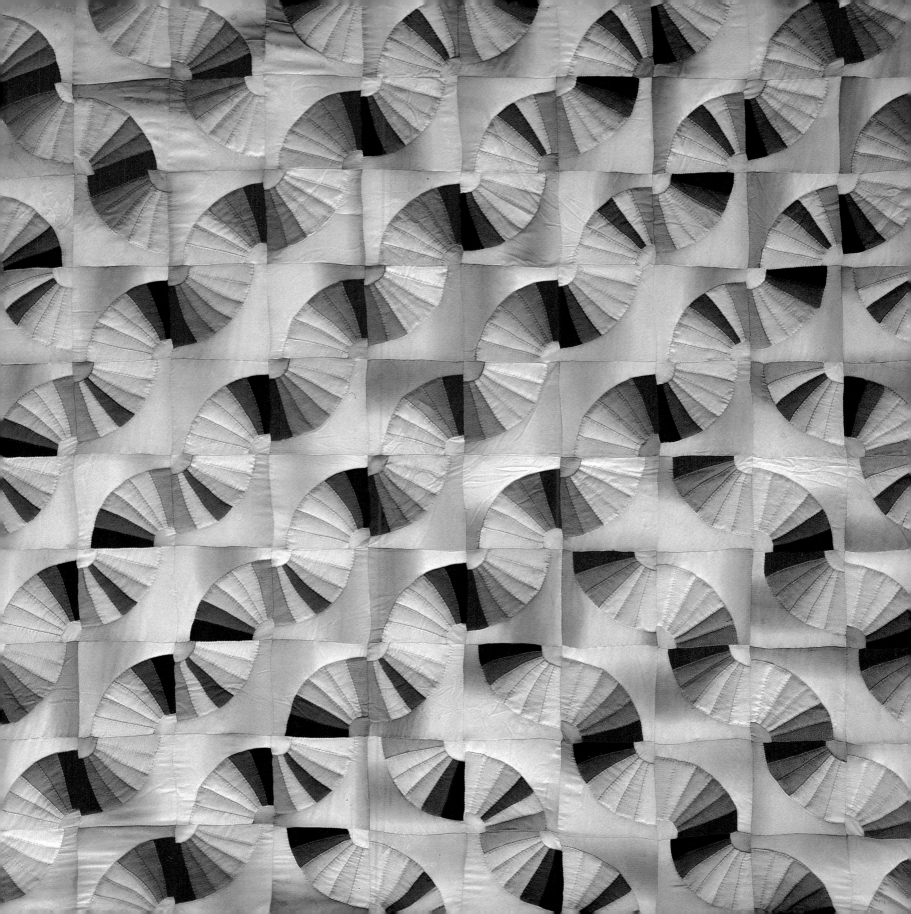

❻ ハッピィネス
Happioess ness
Bonheur
2270 x 2500mm

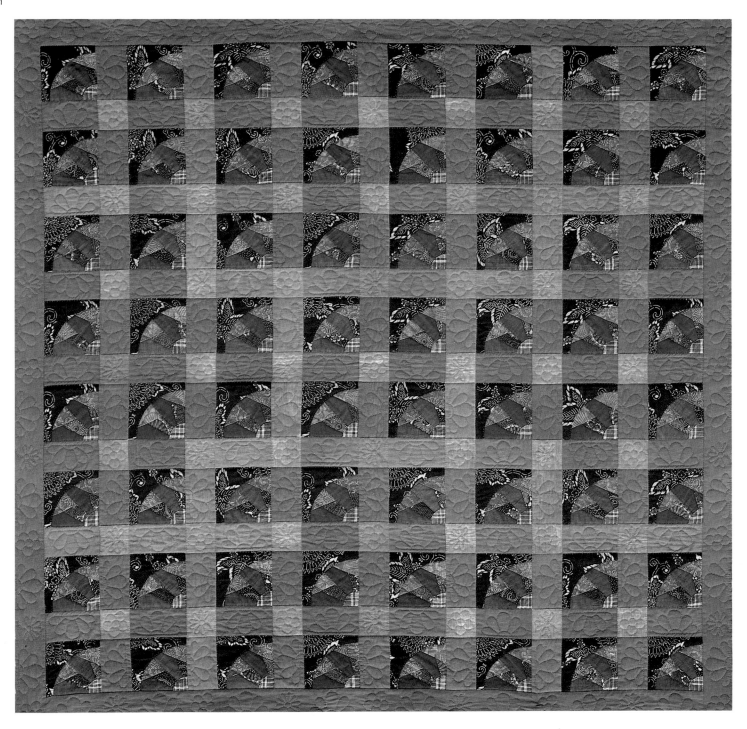

❻ 古里追想
Nostalgia
Nostalgie
1930 x 1930mm

❻❸ 氾　濫
Flood
Raz-de-marée
2000 x 2000mm

64 光と海
Sea and rays
Mer et lumière
1200 x 1550mm

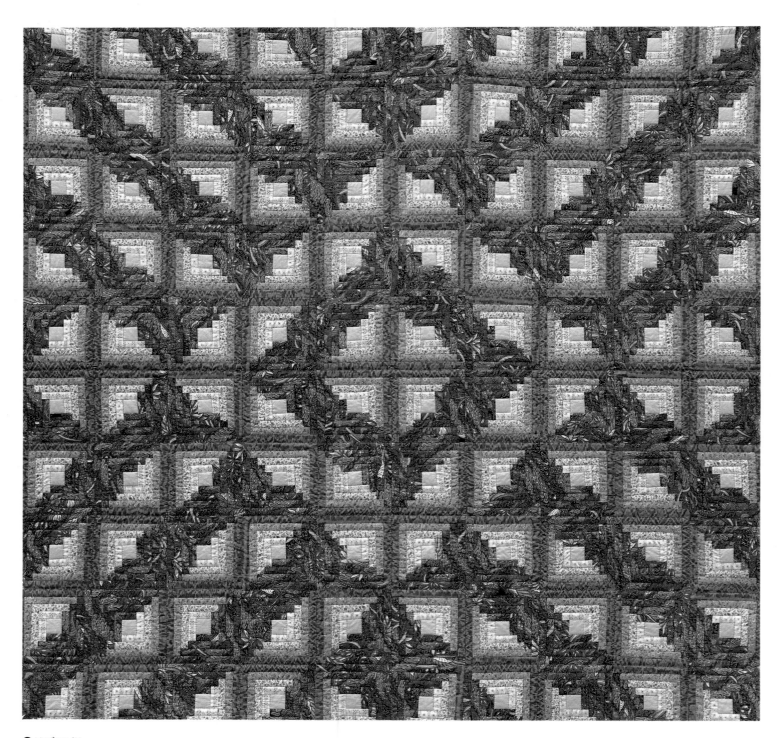

❻❺ はびこる根

Spreading roots

Racines tentaculaires

2000 x 2000mm

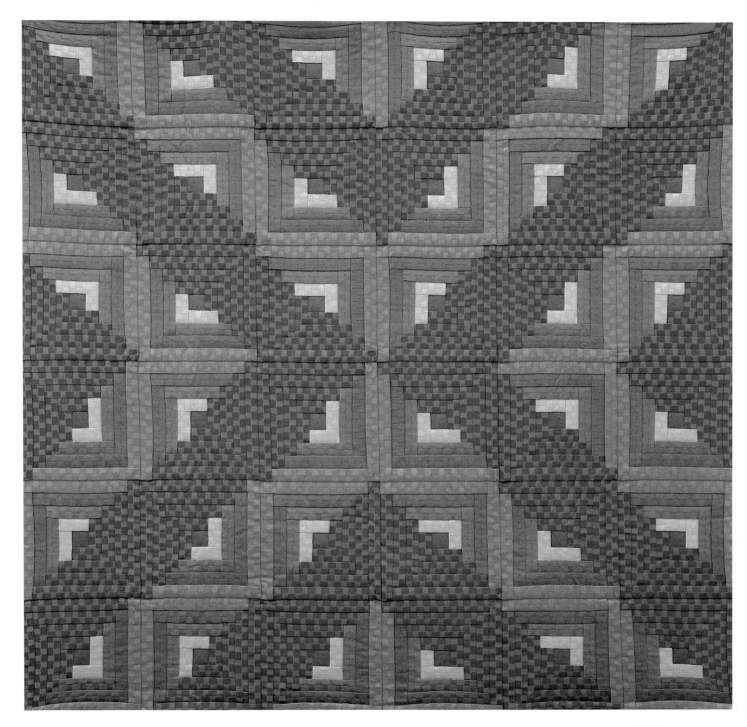

66 開 墾
Reclamation
Conquête
2200 x 2230mm

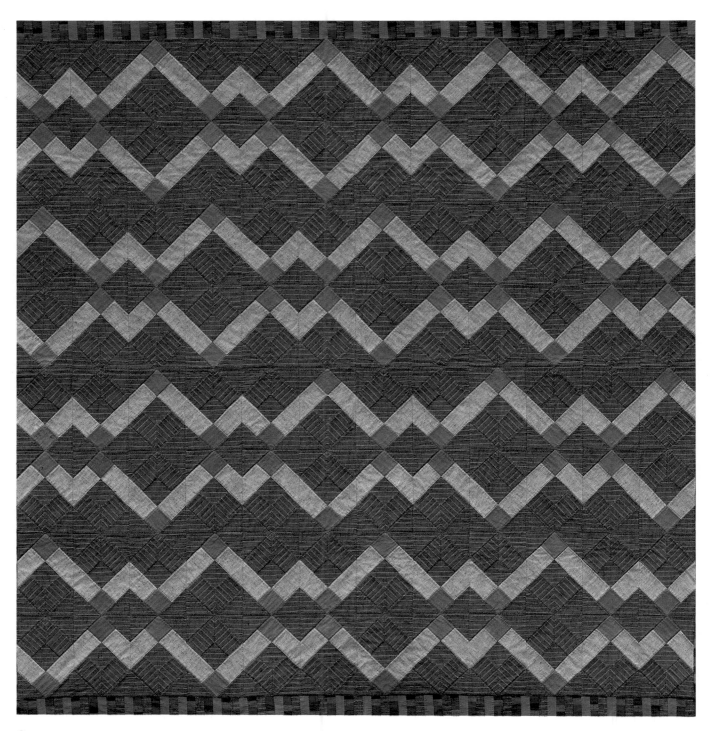

❻❼ フェンス
Fence
Clôture
1850 x 1850mm

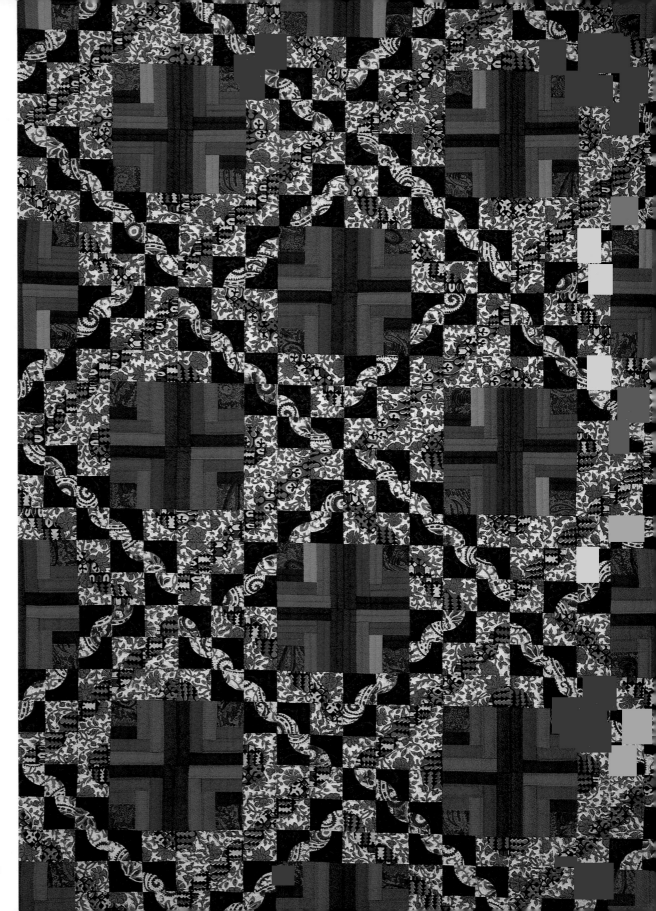

❻❽ 脱　出
Escape
Liberté
1900 x 1300mm

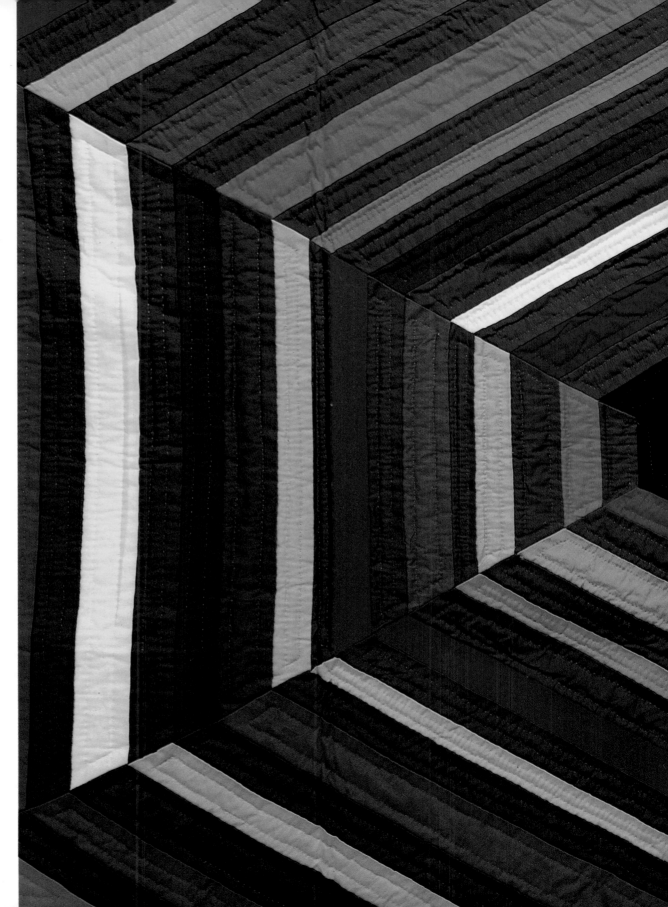

❻⓽ 曲　面
Phases
760 x 1050mm

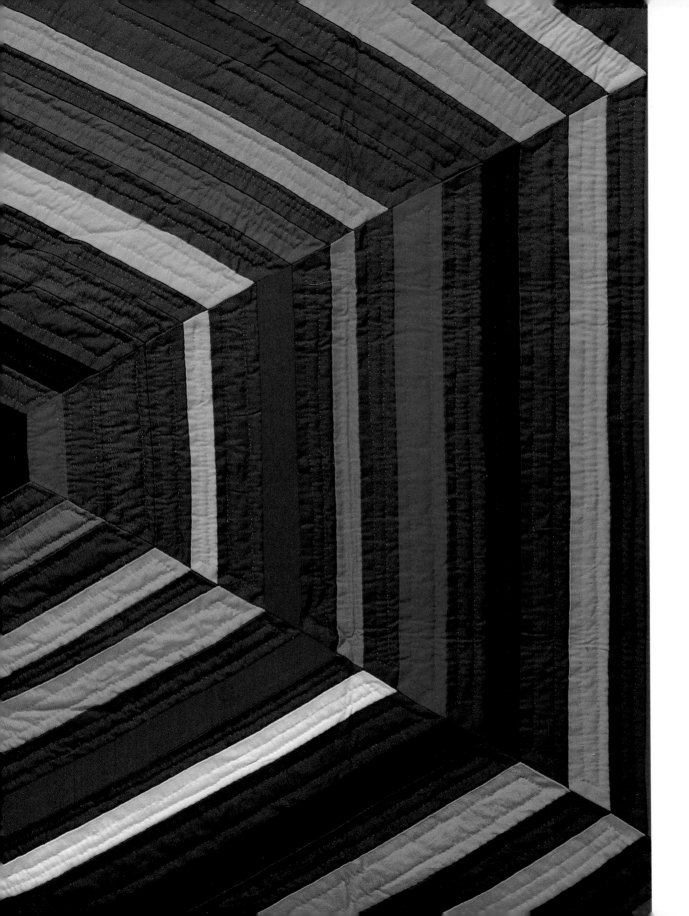

⑦蒼 茫
Dark imarge in blue
Image obscure et gaie

⑦星 斗
Twinkling stars
Etoiles brillantes
2100 x 1800mm

花達の囁き
Flowers whispering
Murmures de fleur

㉓無　題
No title
Non titré

㉔ 無 題
No title
Non titré
2600 x 2400

㉕ 珊瑚礁
Coral reef
Récif de corail
2400 x 2700mm

❼❻ 光 芒
Glory
Gloire
1900 x 1600

⓱ 宝石の涙
Jewel tears
Larmes de bijoux
1550 x 1130mm

Buon Natale

Bonne Année

Gelukkig

Joyeux Noël

Fröhliche Weihnachten

Feliz Natal

Wesolych Swiat

Vrolijk Kerstfeest

Glückliches Neues Jahr

Felices Naviad

Prospero Año Nuevo

Merry Christmas

Happy New Year

⑧ 夢物語 I　Fantastic story-I　Histoire fantastique-I　1750 x 820mm

⑧ 夢物語 II　Fantastic story-II　Histoire fantastique-II　1750 x 820mm

㉜ 夢物語Ⅲ　Fantastic story-Ⅲ　Histoire fantastique-Ⅲ　1710 x 870mm

㉝ 夢物語Ⅳ　Fantastic story-Ⅳ　Histoire fantastique-Ⅳ　1680 x 770mm

❽❹群
Crowd
Foule
830 x 1070mm

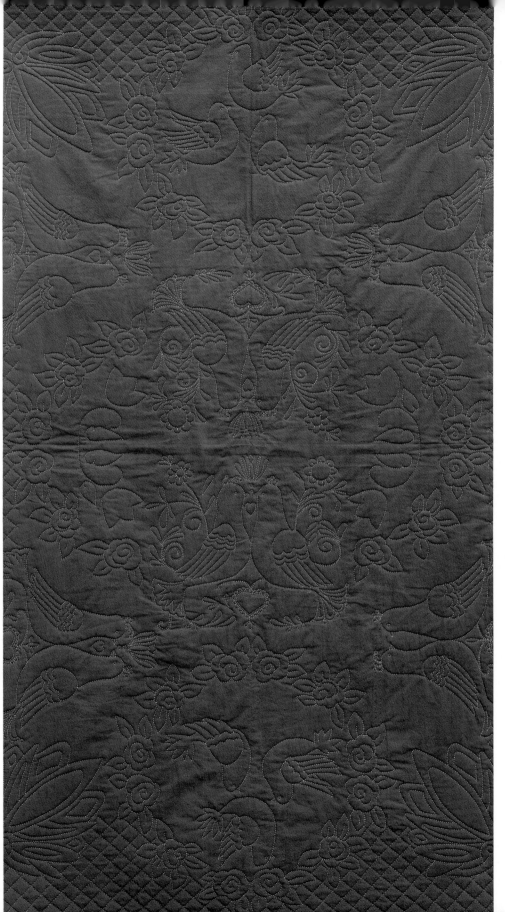

⑧楽　園
Paradise
Paradis
800 x 1400mm

あとがき

　知人であり、今回の作品撮影を担当していただいた写真家の兼本氏から、出版社のオーナー、本田氏とグラフィックデザイナーの大髙猛先生を紹介されたのは、昨年9月初めだった。7月から8月まで目黒の病院に強制入院させられ、退院後の間もない私にとっては予期せぬ出逢いであった。これをきっかけに、又、意欲的に作品に取り組み、デモンストレーションとして、昨年秋、広島のギャラリーで「キルト・アート展」を開催し盛況に終わったのも、かつて私が中国新聞文化センターで講師を勤めたころお世話になった広瀬女史、新聞社文化部デスクの岡山氏等のお力もある。又、作品をきびしく批評し、力づけてくださる広島の中野さん（元画廊経営）や良きブレーンの方々、友人、制作協力をいただいたSEGAWA.P.Q.M.A.のスタッフ一同のバックアップは非常に大きいといえよう。ご多忙の折、快く序文をお引き受けくださった、共立女子大学の北村教授、グラフィックデザイナーの大髙先生や、大阪での活動の場を提供してくださった株式会社松山さん、写真家の兼本先生、光村推古書院の本田氏はじめ、スタッフの皆さまに紙面を借りてお礼申し上げます。

せがわ　せつこ

製作協力

SEGAWA P.Q.M.A. 講師　順不同

清川八寿美　　松浦正子　　小松　冴　　鐘江正代　　是松多鶴子
魚谷牧子　　　加茂サチ子　八田由紀子　数本正子　　藤原ウタコ
湯本まちこ　　近藤裕子　　大原素子

SEGAWA P.Q.M.A. 会員　五十音順

合庭房子　　　有沢玲子　　石山豊美　　内田美智子　大北紋美代
大塚みさよ　　梶河泰子　　金井泰子　　河崎弘子　　川村登久子
岸上良子　　　喜多村淑　　郡司祥子　　神山かをり　後藤智子
清水由美子　　杉本久栄　　高田恵美子　高橋真美　　竹澤妙子
竹原京子　　　竹安美知子　椿原克都子　寺嶋輝子　　遠山結子
中出満江　　　野中悦子　　花田奈美子　樋口仁美　　平田貴美
藤井民江　　　仏石紘子　　南口恵美子　六岡京子　　龍　純子

東京都目黒区下目黒1-2-14　ブルーストーンハイム102
03(779)4242
大阪市南区心斎橋筋2-12　小大丸ビル1F　松山内
06(211)7835
広島市安佐南区沼田町伴700-240　是松方
082(848)1642
福岡市中央区舞鶴1-2-33　ライオンズマンション404
092(714)5728　（火曜日）

Profile

Born in 1946.
Graduated Tama Arts University. Later, studied graphic design, textile, interior display and flower design in Europe. Presently head of SEGAWA P.Q.M.A. (Patchwork Quilt Association), she is teaching at Tokyo, Osaka, Hiroshima, Fukuoka and other places. She is also active as a professional interior coordinator and flower designer.